A LOOK AT PRIMARY SOURCES

NEWSPAPERS

BY KRISTEN RAJCZAK NELSON

...SH AS TITANIC SINKS; ON...
...TLY WOMEN AND CHILDREN

CAPTAIN E. J. SMITH ON THE BRIDGE OF THE TITANIC.
Although wireless reports are silent, it is believed he went down with his ship.

THE TITANIC, THE GREATEST STEAMSHIP EVER BUILT, WHICH FOUNDERED ON HER FIRST TRANSATLANTIC VOYAGE.

NAMES OF SURVIVORS ON THE CARPATHIA

Wireless Brings Partial List of First Cabin Passengers Saved from Titanic.

"LOSS 1,800 SOULS," OLYMPIC'S MESSAGE

Belief Here That Estimated Number Is Too Large by 300---Rescuers Find Wreckage.

The text of the message from the steamer Olympic reporting the sinking of the Titanic and the rescue of 675 survivors, which reached here late last night, also expressed the opinion that 1,800 lives were lost.

"Loss likely total 1,800 souls," the dispatch said in its concluding sentence.

It is hoped and believed here that this is an error, unless the Titanic had more passengers on board than was reported. She carried about 2,200 persons, including passengers and crew. Deducting 675, the known saved, would indicate a loss of more than 1,500 persons.

The Olympic's dispatch follows:

"Carpathia reached Titanic position at daybreak; found boats and wreckage only. Titanic sank about 2:20 a. m., in 41:16 N., 50:14 W. All her boats accounted for, containing about 675 souls saved, crew and ...

The White Star liner Titanic sank at 2:2... 1,150 miles east of Sandy Hook.

First reports placed the number of survivor... at 675. At 2:30 o'clock this morning a dispatch ... said the number aboard the Carpathia was 866.

A still later dispatch said that the Allan Line ... probably picked up some of the victims.

P. A. S. Franklin, vice-president of the In... Marine Company, admitted last night that prob... more than 2,200 souls on the lost vessel were sa... more than 1,500 persons went down with her.

MOSTLY WOMEN AND CHI...

TITANIC TWO MILES DEEP | $600,000 IN PEARLS ABOARD

Gareth Stevens PUBLISHING
CRASHCOURSE

Please visit our website, www.garethstevens.com. For a free color catalog of all our high-quality books, call toll free 1-800-542-2595 or fax 1-877-542-2596.

Cataloging-in-Publication Data

Names: Nelson, Kristen Rajczak.
Title: Newspapers / Kristen Rajczak Nelson.
Description: New York : Gareth Stevens, 2024. | Series: A look at primary sources | Includes glossary, index, and bibliographic information
Identifiers: ISBN 9781538287521 (pbk) | ISBN 9781538287538 (library bound) | ISBN 9781538287545 (ebook)
Subjects: LCSH: Journalism--Juvenile literature | Information resources-- Juvenile literature | Newspapers-- Juvenile literature
Classification: LCC PN4731 N45 2024 | DDC 070.1/72--dc24

First Edition

Published in 2024 by
Gareth Stevens Publishing
2544 Clinton Street
Buffalo, NY 14224

Designer: Claire Wrazin
Editor: Kristen Rajczak Nelson

Photo credits: Cover (photo), pp. 11, 15, 19, 29 Courtesy of Library of Congress; series art (background texture) Verbena/Shutterstock.com; series art (cover typeface) Gleb Guralnyk/Shutterstock.com; p. 5 magicoven/Shutterstock.com; p. 7 Ground Picture/Shutterstock.com; series art (photo frame) Nataliia K/Shutterstock.com; p. 9 Joseph Sohm/Shutterstock.com; pp. 11, 13 (hand drawn circle) Maxger/Shutterstock.com; p. 13 Kaspars Grinvalds/Shutterstock.com; p. 17 (Washington Post) File:Wash_Post_cover_page_Aug_9_1925_cover_page.jpg/Wikimedia Commons; p. 17 (Wall Street Journal) File:WSJ_July_2_1889_front_page.jpg/Wikimedia Commons; p. 21 File:1887_theatre_ads_BostonDailyGlobe22May.jpg/Shutterstock.com; p. 23 James E. Knopf/Shutterstock.com; p. 23 (arrows) Lyudmyla Ishchenko/Shutterstock.com; p. 25 Stock-Asso/Shutterstock.com; p. 27 sebra/Shutterstock.com.

Printed in the United States of America

CPSIA compliance information: Batch #CS24GS: For further information contact Gareth Stevens at 1-800-542-2595.

CONTENTS

Words in the glossary appear in **bold** type the first time they are used in the text.

HEADING INTO HISTORY

Newspapers were the best source of **information** for hundreds of years! They are often primary sources. A primary source gives firsthand facts. It may have been created, or made, during a time period being studied. It may have been created by someone who **witnessed** an event.

MAKE THE GRADE

Many newspapers had a morning and evening **edition**. The evening edition often updated stories from the morning!

USEFUL SOURCE

Newspapers can also be secondary sources. A secondary source is something that offers **interpretation** or comments about a primary source or event. Depending on the kind of research, or study, it is used for, the same newspaper could be used as either a primary or a secondary source!

MAKE THE GRADE

Before the internet, newspapers might have been the only way people in an area found out what was going on in the wider world!

WITNESS TO HISTORY

There's no question that a newspaper article, or story, is a primary source when it is an eyewitness account. The **journalist** has written about something they saw. They may write about what it was like to be in a city where an attack occurred.

MAKE THE GRADE

A news article that gives quotes from people who witnessed an event is also a primary source. "Quotes" are exactly what a person said.

Newspapers are primary sources when used to research a time period. Someone may look to Greensboro, North Carolina, newspapers from 1960 to learn more about the historic **sit-in** there. A newspaper article written today about the same event would be a secondary source.

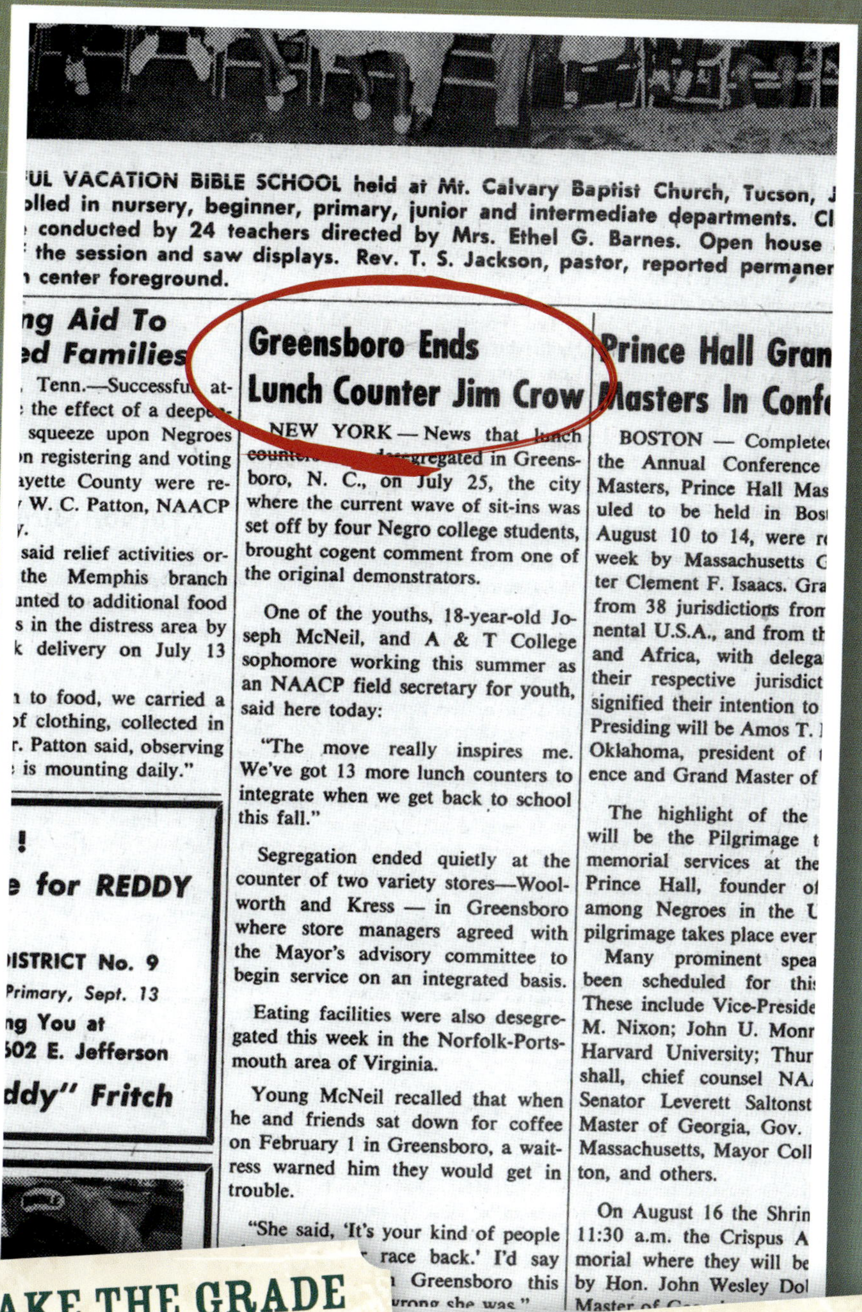

ʼUL VACATION BIBLE SCHOOL held at Mt. Calvary Baptist Church, Tucson, J
olled in nursery, beginner, primary, junior and intermediate departments. Cl
conducted by 24 teachers directed by Mrs. Ethel G. Barnes. Open house
the session and saw displays. Rev. T. S. Jackson, pastor, reported permaner
n center foreground.

ng Aid To
ed Families

Tenn.—Successfu at-
the effect of a deepe
squeeze upon Negroes
n registering and voting
ayette County were re-
W. C. Patton, NAACP

said relief activities or-
the Memphis branch
unted to additional food
s in the distress area by
k delivery on July 13

n to food, we carried a
of clothing, collected in
r. Patton said, observing
is mounting daily."

!
e for REDDY
ISTRICT No. 9
Primary, Sept. 13
ng You at
502 E. Jefferson
ddy" Fritch

Greensboro Ends Lunch Counter Jim Crow

NEW YORK — News that lunch counters desegregated in Greensboro, N. C., on July 25, the city where the current wave of sit-ins was set off by four Negro college students, brought cogent comment from one of the original demonstrators.

One of the youths, 18-year-old Joseph McNeil, and A & T College sophomore working this summer as an NAACP field secretary for youth, said here today:

"The move really inspires me. We've got 13 more lunch counters to integrate when we get back to school this fall."

Segregation ended quietly at the counter of two variety stores—Woolworth and Kress — in Greensboro where store managers agreed with the Mayor's advisory committee to begin service on an integrated basis.

Eating facilities were also desegregated this week in the Norfolk-Portsmouth area of Virginia.

Young McNeil recalled that when he and friends sat down for coffee on February 1 in Greensboro, a waitress warned him they would get in trouble.

"She said, 'It's your kind of people ... race back.' I'd say ... Greensboro this ... wrong she was."

Prince Hall Gran
Masters In Conf

BOSTON — Complete
the Annual Conference
Masters, Prince Hall Mas
uled to be held in Bos
August 10 to 14, were r
week by Massachusetts G
ter Clement F. Isaacs. Gra
from 38 jurisdictions from
nental U.S.A., and from th
and Africa, with delega
their respective jurisdict
signified their intention to
Presiding will be Amos T.
Oklahoma, president of
ence and Grand Master of

The highlight of the
will be the Pilgrimage t
memorial services at the
Prince Hall, founder of
among Negroes in the U
pilgrimage takes place ever
Many prominent spea
been scheduled for thi
These include Vice-Preside
M. Nixon; John U. Monr
Harvard University; Thur
shall, chief counsel NA
Senator Leverett Saltonst
Master of Georgia, Gov.
Massachusetts, Mayor Coll
ton, and others.

On August 16 the Shrin
11:30 a.m. the Crispus A
morial where they will be
by Hon. John Wesley Dol

MAKE THE GRADE

The 1960 sit-in in Greensboro included students protesting, or standing against, **segregation** at a local lunch counter.

SHOWING PERSPECTIVES

A point of view is the way someone thinks or looks at something. Newspapers can be primary sources that show points of view, or perspectives. An article may show the point of view of the writer, a group of people, or a community at large.

MAKE THE GRADE

Newspaper articles that are written to give a point of view, or opinion, on a topic are called editorials or columns. These may be found in the opinion section of the newspaper.

Journalists often try to make their work objective. This means they present facts without their own feelings or ideas. However, as long as newspapers have been around, there has been bias. Bias is the personal judgments someone has.

MARYLAND SUFFRAGE NEWS

SUPPLEMENT TO THE WOMAN'S JOURNAL

VOL. I No. 1 | SATURDAY, APRIL 6, 1912 | FIVE CENTS

OUR DEDICATION.

To the poor women without homes, to the little toilers who should be in the schools and playgrounds, to the white slaves in their tragic bondage, and to the children who die, these pages are dedicated! May every woman who is not too idle to have a thought, or too vain to have a soul, or too rich in gold to have a heart, join in the great struggle for women's freedom!

Purity, Liberty, Justice — these we must work for!

THE LAMP OF SACRIFICE

Have you ever thought how much money has been spent by men in their great wars for political freedom? No great revolution ever has or ever can be carried through successfully without money to sustain the soldiers and to pay for the supplies. We need $30,000 this year for the work in Maryland. Our woman soldiers cannot enlist unless a living wage is insured to them. Traveling in the counties is expensive. Printing and advertising cannot be done for nothing. Meetings must be held, and they cost money. Sacrifice, personal sacrifice, has been at the root of every great social reform. *What will you give?*

Our task is to educate one-quarter of a million voters in the principles of Justice and Righteousness. What will *you* contribute toward their instruction?

Give to the Suffrage work now, and we can win the battle quickly. Wait, and the work waits with you.

Every penny counts. Give what you can. Give the most you can. Give until you feel it. We want a contribution from every Suffragist in the State in our war chests, and we want the gold sanctified by the spirit of self-sacrifice.

Give to the Suffrage work now to the end that you may give effectively to the philanthropies when the vote is won. Many of the charities we are now supporting will not be needed when the humanitarian instincts of women have full scope in the government. To give to the Suffrage work now is the surest, safest, most effective way of giving to the poor.

THE HEARING

On Which Side Do You Stand?

THE HEARING AT ANNAPOLIS

Suffragists and Antis Should Read This Report Carefully. It Will Help the Former to Understand the Opposition and Will Convert the Latter Into Suffragists

The complete stenographic report of the proceedings on the floor of the House of Delegates when the State-wide Bill was voted upon will be published serially in the MARYLAND SUFFRAGE NEWS, with a running commentary by way of explanation of certain moves and counter-moves on the part of the Delegates.

In this first number attention must be called especially to the preliminary words of Messrs. Campbell, Waters and Cummings because of their bearing on the trivial, but somewhat notorious, event known as the Waters episode. The daily press has already given an account of the way in which Mrs. Hooker rudely refused to shake hands with Mr. Waters after his speech on the floor of the House. It has been explained that this arbitrary action on the part of Mrs. Hooker was at least due in part to the fact that Mr. Waters

nal unlimited bill, and it was probably for this reason that they did not wish to have that amendment reported out. As soon as Mr. Campbell's motion was before the House, Messrs. Cummings, Marbury and Waters were seen hastily to get together with the obvious purpose of determining upon some counter-move which would put Mr. Campbell at a loss. Undoubtedly, it was then decided that Mr. Waters should take up the cudgels against the bill, and it is at least reasonable to suppose that he may explain his apparent lack of faith by the fact that, when the bill came up for discussion, it was not the bill that he had anticipated having before the House. Possibly he meant in his previous statement that he would simply not oppose Bill No. 13, since he thought it had no chance at all of passage. The first remark of Mr. Waters—

MEETING AT WEST PARK RECREATION CENTER

The meeting at West Park Recreation Center, March 25, was a thoroughly enthusiastic one. Dr. Anna H. Shaw made the speech of the evening and was at her best. Her remarks teemed with wit and her audience, though for the most part Suffragists who are accused by the Antis to be woefully lacking in the much-to-be-desired sense of humor, was thoroughly appreciative.

At the beginning of her talk Dr. Shaw was presented with a handsome bouquet of white roses and carnations. In accepting it she remarked that in the earlier days of woman suffrage it was not bouquets that usually came to the platform. She pointed out that a common criticism of Suffragists was, that they wanted to be like men, though just why they should want to be like them she could not understand.

Later on in her remarks she brought out the fact that, whenever men wanted to decide a very important question or be extremely dignified, they first put on a gown, adding that no sculptor

CALL FOR VOLUNTEERS

ENLIST IN THE SERVICE.

By this time we have had ample opportunity to learn that there is no use in trying to persuade the delegates to give votes to women. We must force them to do what we know to be right, and the only way in which we can do this is to organize a strong "Woman's Party," that will first pave the way to votes for women, and which will serve afterwards as a strong, closely-welded force for civic righteousness. Once organized, we can get behind all sorts of good movements and hasten their success. And so, if we spend the next two years in perfecting our political organization, we need not waste sighs over our recent defeat. We can make up for lost time through our organization when the vote is won.

The plan is extremely simple: The legislative district or county, the ward and the precinct are the units. There must be a chairman for the legislative district or county, a ward leader for each ward or district in the counties, and a precinct leader for each precinct. When the work in the precinct developes we can arrange it according to the block system, as the political parties do. Each precinct leader or captain must keep a complete list of the Suffragists in her precinct, and give a duplicate of this list to the ward leader, who, in her turn, will send duplicates to headquarters for proper filing. The ward leader must have as many little books as there are precincts in her ward, and keep her lists each in its own precinct book. Each precinct leader must, of course, have her own duplicate book. Then, every month a meeting of the ward and precinct leaders must be held in each ward to report progress and to initiate plans of campaign. The progress, of course, will be dependent entirely on the number of voters secured who are willing to sign pledge cards stating that they will vote in the primaries only for suffrage candidates. The district chairman and the ward leaders will act merely as the organizers of the work, and do no personal canvassing themselves. The precinct captains will do practically nothing but canvassing. In this

MAKE THE GRADE

A whole newspaper may be known for a certain bias, such as supporting women's suffrage, or the right to vote.

When using a newspaper as a primary source, look for bias. Sometimes, facts will have been left out of stories to support a bias. Other times, some facts may be wrong. Newspaper articles from history can be checked against other sources to find the truth.

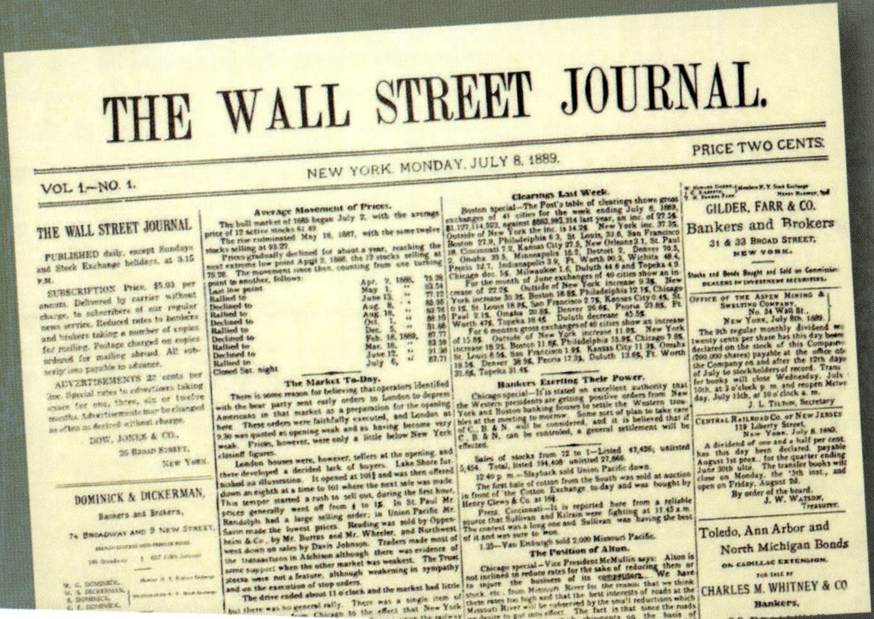
THE WALL STREET JOURNAL.

NEW YORK. MONDAY, JULY 8, 1889.

PRICE TWO CENTS.

VOL. 1.—NO. 1.

THE WALL STREET JOURNAL

PUBLISHED daily, except Sundays and Stock Exchange holidays, at 3:15 P.M.

DOW, JONES & CO., 26 Broad Street, New York.

DOMINICK & DICKERMAN, Bankers and Brokers, 74 Broadway and 9 New Street.

Average Movement of Prices.

The Market To-Day.

Clearings Last Week.

Bankers Exerting Their Power.

The Position of Alton.

GILDER, FARR & CO. Bankers and Brokers, 31 & 33 Broad Street, New York.

Toledo, Ann Arbor and North Michigan Bonds

CHARLES M. WHITNEY & CO. Bankers.

The Washington Post.

WASHINGTON: SUNDAY, AUGUST 9, 1925—EIGHTY-SIX PAGES

FIVE CENTS.

Weather—Local thunder-showers today; tomorrow generally fair; not much change in temperature. Temperature yesterday—Highest, 89; lowest, 66.

CITY GROUPS URGE TELLING NATION OF ADVANTAGES HERE

Million In Population Soon Predicted From Publicity Drive.

COMFORT AND BEAUTY OF HOMES NOTABLE

Bringing Conventions Especially Favored to Advance City's Unique Feature.

Washington, as a good place to live in, will reach a population of a million when efforts to "sell" it to the nation as Florida and California have been "sold" materialize, according to civic and business leaders, who are making an exhaustive study of the possibilities.

These men believe that it will not be long before Americans throughout the States will realize the desirability of living in Washington. For a long time now, they say, these folks throughout the nation have been in the habit of regarding the National Capital merely as a stopping off place—a place to go sightseeing or a place where Congress debates all winter.

Contrary to popular belief, a canvas of leading citizens shows, Washington is a city of homes—grand ones—humble ones—but mostly just comfortable, simple-

PENNSYLVANIA AVENUE MASS OF WHITE DURING KLANSMEN'S PARADE.

The white-gowned ... virtually covered Pennsylvania avenue during yesterday's parade. Photo- ... turning south into Fifteenth street.

(c) Henry Miller News Picture Service, Inc.

WHITE-ROBED KLAN CHEERED ON MARCH IN NATION'S CAPITAL

Police Estimate 30,000 to 35,000 Take Part in Demonstration.

PRAYER FAILS TO HALT RAIN AS PARADE ENDS

Thousands at Monument Rush to Shelter; Some Remain Through Downpour.

AIR OF TENSITY MARKS START OF PROCESSION

Friendly Reception, However, Given to Klansmen of East, South and West.

Phantom-like hosts of the Ku Klux Klan spread their white robe over the nation's most historic thoroughfare yesterday in one of the greatest demonstrations this city has even known.

Appearing, it seemed, from the very shadows of the Capitol, reared in the full majesty of a bright sun, they swept over the wide spaces of the

MAKE THE GRADE

Some newspapers are known for supporting certain **political** ideas.

ABOUT THE TIME

Newspapers are primary sources one might use to see change over time. Their advertisements can show price changes on clothes, homes, and cars. **Advice** columns can show what people thought were problems, answers to those problems, and how both changed over the years.

MAKE THE GRADE

Dear Abby is an advice column that began in 1959. It's still being written today! The kinds of questions asked have changed as communities' concerns have changed.

DEAR ABBY . . .

By ABIGAIL VAN BUREN

Further Your Education, Honey!

DEAR ABBY: For a 23-year-old college graduate I guess I'm pretty stupid, but here's my situation: Last year I met a very attractive man of 29. He told me from the start he'd been keeping company for several years with a woman a little older than himself, and he had no intention of severing their relationship. From all appearances their "relationship" included everything but the marriage license.

I have fallen head over heels in love with him and would give anything to have him for myself. He says he "loves" me but he loves her, too. He sees me on Tuesdays, Fridays and every other Sunday. It kills me to know he is with her when he's not with me. I can't give him up and can't live without him. Is there a solution?

HOPELESSLY IN LOVE.

You can live without him and you'll probably have to, so save yourself further agony and call it quits while you still have your youth. Your Romeo wants to eat his cake and have it, too. Give him the "frosting" he so properly deserves.

* * * *

DEAR ABBY: Isn't it considered proper etiquette for a person who is entering a room to say, "Good morning" (or "Good evening," whichever the case may be?) rather than for the person who is already in the room to say it first? This has bothered me for years because I was taught that the person entering the room should greet those already there. Some people don't know this apparently.

IRRITATED.

Common sense is the best rule. Before the silence becomes awkward, say "hello" and to heck with what's proper.

* * * *

DEAR ABBY: My mother-in-law is the sweetest, most wonderful person in the world—when she isn't drinking. Lately, she is so loaded by noon every day you can't reason with her. The worst part of it is that no one in her family thinks this is a problem. They say, "Ma's feeling good," and will even have one with her any time of the night or day.

I want to help her because she is getting worse. My husband travels and doesn't seem to realize how serious it is, and her other children think I'm a busybody. Can you help me help her?

WORRIED.

Investigate "Al Anon"—a branch of Alcoholics Anonymous, whose purpose it is to teach the families and friends of alcoholics how to cope with them.

* * * *

For a personal reply, send a self-addressed, envelope to ABBY, i… The Evening …

Wh… Ab… …

Program Planned

A peak into Wright's "Cra… board" will be … at the United S… Health Service… Wives Club wher… for luncheon at … day at the Nav… Club in Bethesda.

Mrs. Wright wi… antique treasures… the colors in a co… living room or set… in a traditional h… discusses antique… teriors. Born in … England, a gra… Queenswood Colleg… fordshire, Mrs. W… acquired a wealth … edge regarding an…

Luncheon hoste… Mrs. L. J. Oliver, M… Bowen, Mrs. J. D. … and Mrs. J. W. Kn…

Ads in newspapers are an important tool to look at how people of a time lived. The kinds of items in ads show what the newspaper knew about its readers. If costly goods were advertised, a newspaper knew its readers had money to spend.

THE BOSTON SUNDAY GLOBE—SUNDAY, MAY 22, 1887—TWENTY PAGES. 11

AUSTIN AND STONE'S MUSEUM.

BOSTON THEATRE

LAST WEEK OF THE GREAT HERRMANN, The World-Renowned Prestidigitator, ASSISTED BY Mme. HERRMANN.

Entire Change of Programme.

NEW FEATURES! NEW MARVELS!

DECAPITATION.

A Man's Head Cut Off in Full View of the Audience!

LITTLE FOLKS MATINEES WEDNESDAY AND SATURDAY.

THE WORLD.

HOWARD ATHENÆUM.

ONE WEEK, Commencing MONDAY, May 23,'87.

THE POPULAR IRISH COMEDIAN, TONY HART,

UNRIVALLED COMEDY COMPANY

DONNYBROOK.

HOLLIS ST. THEATRE.

RICE'S BEAUTIFUL EVANGELINE.

60 ARTISTS 60

GLOBE THEATRE.

GILBERT AND SULLIVAN OPERA SEASON.

MIKADO,

BIJOU

2 Performances Daily. 2

LITTLE EM'LY,

A LITTLE LADY

20, 30 & 50c.

WINDSOR THEATRE,

THIS WEEK A GENUINE NOVELTY.

KITTIE POWERS,

NUGGET NELL,

LONE PINE!

WINDSOR THEATRE

TONIGHT,

Boston Theatre.

LECTURE WILLIAM O'BRIEN,

WORLD'S MUSEUM,

CROCODILES

NOT DEAD

THE TIGERS

THE STAGE

THE HALLS.

TRACY AND EGAN

JOSEPH A. KELLEY.

MONS. CICUERE,

MUSICAL DALE,

ED. H. BANKER.

MY COMPANY,

THE DARK-EYED WIDOW.

10 CENTS

Decoration Day,

Melville Garden,

EDMANDS' BAND

Refreshments for Sale

FAIRY

LUCY.

WHAT IS IT?

OAKLAND GARDEN.

BOSTON MUSEUM.

AUGUSTIN DALY'S COMPANY,

THE TAMING OF THE SHREW,

AUSTIN'S

Prof. C. A. ROGERS' MAMMOTH

PURITAN

BALLOON,

PEOPLE'S ENTERTAINMENT SOCIETY OF BOSTON.

COCKEREL HALL,

MELVILLE GARDEN,

PARK THEATRE.

WOMAN SUFFRAGE.

GRAND CONCERT

BATTLE OF GETTYSBURG,

BASE BALL.

BOSTON DAILY GLOBE
THEATER ADS
MAY 2, 1887

MAKE THE GRADE

The size, number, and placement of stories and ads can tell what the newspaper thought was most important to its readers.

HISTORIANS' SOURCE

A historian is a person who studies history. They use primary sources to find out the details, or small facts, of historical time periods and events. They often use historical newspapers in their research. They look at and compare different newspapers in their work.

MAKE THE GRADE

Some historical newspapers can be found online. But, more are still found on **microfilm**. Historians must visit libraries and schools in person to see those.

MICROFILM ROLL

When historians consider newspaper stories as primary sources, they must consider the whole newspaper. One article from history cannot be looked at on its own. Historians look at where it was placed in the newspaper. They consider if it was a continuing story.

MAKE THE GRADE

Historians use many newspaper articles about an event or topic together to get a picture of what happened. Sometimes the facts are different!

NEWSPAPERS TODAY

Does your town have a newspaper? Some don't have a paper newspaper anymore! But, there are still many newspapers found online. These online stories can be considered primary sources in many of the same ways as historical newspapers.

MAKE THE GRADE

Today, it's common for a writer's biases to be known, even outside the opinion section.

IMPORTANT SOURCE

Newspapers are records of history that have many parts. Considering a newspaper as a primary source takes time and practice. It's worth it! They offer many details about history and life in the past we might not otherwise know.

The Evening Star.

WITH SUNDAY MORNING EDITION

WASHINGTON, D. C., WEDNESDAY, JANUARY 3, 1923—THIRTY-TWO PAGES. TWO CENTS.

Closing N. Y. Stocks and Bonds, Page 24

"From Press to Home Within the Hour"

Yesterday's Net Circulation, 91,033

FRENCH SPURN BRITISH PLAN ON REPARATIONS; GLOOM AS BREAK NEARS

Poincare Told to Stand Firm by Cabinet.

PREMIERS SEEK TO SHIFT BLAME

Parley Split-Up May Come During This Afternoon.

AMERICA'S HAND SEEN AS GUIDING LAUSANNE PARLEY

While Conference Marks Time, Influence of U. S. Conciliates Delegates.

Germans May Not Present Proposals.

"REVENGE WAR" IS RIDICULED

U.S.-English Pledges to France Held to Be O. K.

FOREIGN AFFAIRS.

Prince Miguel, Pretender's Son, Sells Insurance

SECRECY MARKS HARVEY PARLEY WITH PRESIDENT

Efforts to Interview Diplomat at White House Foiled by Officials.

AMBASSADOR EXPECTED TO CALL UPON HUGHES

BURSUM PENSION MEASURE VETOED

Author of Bill Will Move to Pass It Over President.

Not a Dry Eye in D. C. Building As Police Move All to Tears

Red-Eyed Clerks Weep Freely and Unshamedly for Half an Hour, But—It Was Tear Gas, Not Pity.

"PADLOCK" DRIVE ON RUM PLANNED

Department of Justice and Drys Confer on Extending Force of Writ.

TESTS ARE SUCCESSFUL

DIM LIGHTS PERIL LIFE IN D. C. STREETS

Motorists and Pedestrians Endangered by Shadows in Some Sections.

D. C. BILL MAY PASS IN HOUSE SATURDAY

Supply Measure for 1924 Is to Be Reported Out Tomorrow.

ASKS FOREIGN AID IN WAR ON "DOPE"

U. S. Would Suppress Narcotics by Co-Operation With Other Governments.

Coue

To Write for The Star

A SERIES of articles specially addressed to the American people, to be published during his stay in this country.

Beginning Next Friday

the articles will appear daily, except Sunday, and can be read in Washington only in

The Evening Star

Activity in Business As Reflected by Advertising in The Star

Total Advertising, 1922	21,659,650 lines
Total Advertising, 1921	21,032,405 lines
Gain	627,245 lines

This tremendous increase of 627,245 lines for the year was divided as follows:

Gain in Display Advertising	272,255 lines
Gain in Classified Advertising	354,990 lines
Total Gain	627,245 lines

Circulation of The Star

Yesterday's Circulation	91,033
Same day last year	89,306
Gain	1,727

$125,000 Urged for Georgetown Postal Station

SICK MAN, TRAPPED, DIES IN BURNING BUILDING

BANKER-PREACHER GIVES $25,000 BOND, LEAVES JAIL

MAKE THE GRADE

Using other primary sources such as letters and photographs along with newspapers can help form a complete picture of an event in history.

USING A NEWSPAPER AS A PRIMARY SOURCE

Visit your local library or the Library of Congress website to find a newspaper from the past.

Look at the front page. Find the following:

- the date
- the location of the paper
- the top stories on the page

What does this tell you about the time period the newspaper could be used as a primary source for?

Choose a story to read. *What is it about? Is it a primary or secondary source as it is written?*

Look at where the story is on the page. *What does that tell you about the importance of or interest in the story?*

Read the story again. *Can you find any bias in it? Is anything said in the article a belief that is different from today?*

Find a modern newspaper and ask the same questions as you did the historical paper. *What differences do you notice between them?*

GLOSSARY

advice: A suggestion given about what someone should do.

edition: The form in which something is published, or put out.

information: Knowledge obtained from study or observation.

interpretation: An explanation of the meaning of something.

journalist: Someone whose job it is to gather, write, edit, or otherwise report news stories.

microfilm: A kind of film on which very small photographs of the printed pages of a newspaper are stored.

political: Having to do with politics, or the activities of the government or government officials.

segregation: The forced separation of races or classes.

sit-in: A protest in which people stay in a place until they are given what they demand.

witness: To see something happen.

FOR MORE INFORMATION

BOOKS

Boswell, Kelly. *Research Primary Source Documents: Diaries, Letters, Journals, and More!*. North Mankato, MN: Pebble, 2019.

Keppeler, Jill. *Newspapers Throughout American History.* New York, NY: Gareth Stevens Publishing, 2020.

WEBSITE

Primary vs. Secondary
umb.libguides.com/PrimarySources/secondary
Compare primary and secondary sources, and find examples of each, on this website.

INDEX